LES FOLLES ALLIÉES PRESENT

A Play

English translation by
Linda Gaboriau

gynergy
books

Originally published in French as *Mademoiselle Autobody* by
les Folles Alliées (les Editions des Folles Alliées, 1987).

Performance Rights
Any requests for the right to perform *Miss Autobody*
in any manner whatsoever should be addressed to
Lucie Godbout, c/o gynergy books.

Edited by: Shelley Tepperman
Cover Photograph: Michel Lemay
Printed and Bound in Canada by: Hignell Printing Limited

*gynergy books acknowledges the generous
support of the Canada Council.*

*Les Folles Alliées would like to thank Le Ministère du conseil exécutif — secrétariat
aux affaires intergouvernementales canadiennes for its generous support.*

Published by
gynergy books
P.O. Box 2023
Charlottetown, P.E.I.
Canada C1A 7N7

Distributors:
Canada: General Publishing
United States: Inland Book Company
United Kingdom: Turnaround Distribution

CANADIAN CATALOGUING IN PUBLICATION DATA
Folles alliées (Theater group)

[Mademoiselle Autobody. English]

Translation of: Mademoiselle Autobody.
ISBN 0-921881-25-8

I. Title. II. Title: Mademoiselle Autobody.
English.

PS8561.045M3313 1993   C842'.54   C93-098686-5
PQ3919.2.F65M3313 1993

I'll consider making porngraphic movies the day I see
some beauty in these films, the day someone tells me
he cried watching one of them.

FEDERICO FELLINI

The release of *Miss Autobody* marks a special occasion for gynergy books — the publication of our first play. There were certainly compelling reasons to undertake this particular project. As a feminist publisher, we are dedicated to the development and promotion of writing by women for women, in its myriad forms. *Miss Autobody* addresses an issue of great importance to us as women and feminists — the insidious effects of pornography on our vision of ourselves as fully human beings. Indeed, although the French edition of *Miss Autobody* was first published in 1987, the subject remains relevant. Over the past five years progress has been made in controlling the distribution of degrading images of women and children, but they are still being produced and are still readily available. This groundbreaking play manages to address such violence against women in a unique, energetic way — through laughter, story and song. And that gives us a third compelling reason for publishing the work: it's a good play — one that can be read with enjoyment and successfully adapted and performed by women everywhere.

We are proud to add *Miss Autobody* to our list, and proud to have a part in translating the inspired spirit of les Folles Alliées — the all-woman Quebec theatre troupe who wrote the play — to English-language audiences. The vitality of the culture out of which this play came, and the importance of the Quebecois contribution to feminist dialogue (for, by virtue of their position within a distinctly different culture, women in Quebec offer the rest of us in North America a unique perspective on feminist issues, and on "difference" in general), cannot be underestimated. Translator Linda Gaboriau has done a wonderful job of preserving the intent and remarkable energy of the original production, while making the play universally accessible to readers and performers. Editor Shelley Tepperman has also used her skills to ensure that the text consistently offers the same seamless accessibility.

It is our hope that this English-language version of *Miss Autobody* will, in the words of the authors, "Make you smile, make you laugh, make you read." To that we add: May it also make you act — on stage or off, against violence towards women.

PREFACE

You are about to read the English translation of a play by les Folles Alliées[1], a women's theatre collective from Quebec. We started out as a group of friends and somewhere along the way we became a professional theatre troupe. We shared ten years of touring, a crazy round of hotels and cafe-theatres, larger and more prestigious theatres, and finally, our last performance in Montreal's biggest cabaret, The Spectrum! Beginning (and ending) with minimal resources, les Folles Alliées made their controversial presence felt in the cultural landscape of Quebec. We always tackled topical subjects involving women, daring to laugh at society's ills, at the failings of both men and women, wanting to make both sides laugh at themselves and each other. Sexist advertising, pornography, fear, lack of financial resources — these issues (and women's fertile imaginations) were part of our reality and became our favourite subjects. For example, we lived in Quebec City where the annual winter carnival brought the inevitable beauty contest, complete with its "Duchesses" and its Carnival Queen. Right up our alley! We wrote a show called *Enfin Duchesses! (Duchesses at Last!)*, in which we were all beauty contest winners who ultimately sabotaged the contest from within!

While on tour with *Enfin Duchesses!*, we were involved in a rather unusual incident. One evening, while enjoying a well-deserved drink after a performance, we lifted our glasses and our eyes, and what did we see on the lounge's TV screen but a porno film. After the nth rape, true to our Pink Brigade selves (and there were a dozen of us), we took action. One of us got up on her chair and, CLICK!, she turned off the

---

1 Translator's note: In spirit and almost literally, Folles Alliées translates as "Crazy Ladies United," but in French there is also a pun based on the fact that the name sounds like the expression "folles à lier," as in "fit to be tied."

TV set, gently but firmly. Provoking, of course, an uproar of protests from three or four guys who felt they were being deprived of their "rights and freedoms" as customers — that is, as males. The discussion was heated. The gentlemen were hurling insults, the debate was lively, to say the least and the owner decided to intervene. But we finally made our point and the TV set stayed off. Moral of the story: twelve beers are worth more than three or four. The waitress, who had stayed out of the altercation, came to see us afterwards and told us how much she appreciated our gesture, especially since she couldn't do a thing about it, for fear of losing her job (which was totally understandable). Several months later, that waitress became Jeannine in *Mademoiselle Autobody*.

From the very first performance, *Mademoiselle Autobody* (alias *Miss Autobody*) was a success, with sold out houses, an extended run and a tour. Yet the play tackles difficult subjects: pornography and violence against women. We believe that the play's success is largely due to its good-natured tone and its risqué humour. And to the fact that *Miss Autobody* is also about love and engines! The set, costumes and sound design (music and noises) indicated in the text help achieve the effect of a live comic strip for adults.

Managing to denounce a situation and make people laugh at the same time is no mean feat. For all of us in les Folles Alliées collective, humour should always be based on the notion of respect. We have great respect for the subjects we tackle and for the characters we play. A member of the Pink Brigade or an old lady can (and should) make us laugh, but never will they make us laugh at them! Borderline? Yes, indeed!

This is why, beneath the seemingly casual tone, every line in the script has been carefully thought through. We attempted to arouse or titillate the "this is outrageous" side of people, rather than their prudish side. Hence the risqué jokes about sex. We wanted to illustrate the deceitful and hateful aspects of pornography. It is deceitful because it gives young men a totally unreal image of women — how will they know how to act when faced with a real woman? It is hateful because women are tortured for the pleasure of voyeurs. There are also the grey areas of soft-core pornography and the exploitation of topless dancers.

Whatever the subject, women are never portrayed as victims in our plays. Whether they're waitresses, topless dancers, or married to consumers of pornography, our characters live their lives with their eyes wide open and they fight to be respected. Our plays are first and foremost for these women. That's why real dancers relate to our work and often ask for a copy of the script so they can use it in dealing with their pimp or boss. We're honoured by these requests and see them as the ultimate recognition of our work. Our theatre is for these women, and for men who don't know a thing about feminism but who understand basic common sense. Our plays weren't aimed at already converted-to-the-cause feminist intellectuals, athough they eventually came to see *Mademoiselle Autobody* and they laughed too.

In *Mademoiselle Autobody* we wanted to show that there is a relationship between the so-called harmless "girlie" magazines, provocative videoclips and topless dancers. These are simply the tips of the iceberg — the hidden glacier which makes our blood run cold is the "snuff" film industry, in which women are monstrously attacked. While the "snuff" industry may have been pushed further underground since this play was first created in 1985, pornography is still very much with us. Progress has been made in controlling its distribution, but there is still a long way to go. Violence and the (ab)use of female sexuality have become so commonplace that we hardly notice them anymore. The result: female stereotypes abound on big and small screens, in magazines, videoclips, advertising etc. While these clichés might drive us to tears in our daily lives, they make fabulous satirical material on stage.

Those interested in producing *Miss Autobody* should investigate the pornographic material available in their own areas. The more relevant to your particular community, the more impact the play will have. So do everything you like to make this piece your own! Don't hesitate to incorporate your local scandals, the latest absurd clichés, and recent news on pornography and violence against women. As well, all the cultural references in this script, ranging from the names of characters and places to the choice of popular songs and videoclips, can and should be adapted and updated. When adapting characters' names, remember that the names of the members of the Pink Brigade all contain the initials B.R. — hence the password and code names.

Have fun performing *Miss Autobody* and shake up those conservative attitudes — it feels great. But be prepared to feel the boat rock. Sometimes it's hard to bear the brunt of controversy. For les Folles Alliées, it has always been a stimulant. Break a leg, as they say, and enjoy!

BRRRRR!
Lucie Godbout, for les Folles Alliées

P.S. Les Folles Alliées are proud to be translated into Shakespeare's mother tongue. Did you know that in his day, women weren't allowed to perform on stage? Well, the tides have turned — we always played the male roles ourselves!

P.P.S. During the original production of *Mademoiselle Autobody*, real Pink Brigades cropped up all over Quebec City and Montreal. Were we part of them? Only our hairdresser knows for sure! We love to keep people guessing. Sometimes there's no distinguishing theatre from real life and that's the way we like it!

PRODUCTION TEAM AND CAST

Miss Autobody (Mademoiselle Autobody) was first produced in Quebec City at the Théâtre du Grand Dérangement on January 30, 1985 by les Folles Alliées Inc. The play was subsequently presented at the Théâtre de la Bordée in Quebec City, the Théâtre d'Aujourd'hui in Montreal, at the Atelier of the National Arts Centre in Ottawa and on tour throughout the province of Quebec.

CAST:

Barbara Robidoux and Timothy	*Hélène Bernier*
Beverley Rioux and Maurice Malo	*Jocelyne Corbeil*
Bibi Rancourt and Mariette Malo	*Pascale Gagnon*
Brigitte Roby and Phéda Simard	*Lucie Godbout*
Béatrice Roberge and Jeannine	*Agnès Maltais*
Keyboards and offstage voices	*Christine Boillat*

Directed by	*Pierrette Robitaille*
Set design by	*Geneviève Gauvreau*
. . . .	*and Monique Dion on tour*
Assisted by	*Caroline Drouin*
. . . .	*and Diane Marier*
. . . .	*and Anne Robert on tour*
Lighting design by	*Aurore Thériault*
. . . .	*and Claude-André Roy for subsequent productions*
Songs written by	*Jocelyne Corbeil*
Composed by	*Jocelyne Corbeil*
. . . .	*and Christine Boillat*
Musical arrangments by	*Christine Boillat*
Press relations and publicity	*Monique Bérubé*
. . . .	*and Christine Gourgue*
Make-up	*Elaine Hamel*
Written by	*les Folles Alliées:*
. . . .	*Hélène Bernier*
. . . .	*Jocelyne Corbeil*
. . . .	*Pascale Gagnon*
. . . .	*Lucie Godbout*
. . . .	*Agnès Maltais*

CHARACTERS

The Pink Brigade (Barbara Robidoux, Beverley Rioux, Brigitte Roby, Beatrice Roberge, Bibi Rancourt) Secret agents with a secret office and a secret telephone number so they can secretly support feminist causes. Look innocent enough, but don't step on their blue suede shoes...

Bibi Rancourt Fine strapping lass. New garage owner in Pompomville. She is the Gretzky of screwdrivers, the Jordan of carburetors. Non-traditional and not the least bit snobbish, but don't step on her blue suede shoes...

Maurice Malo Mariette's husband, Stephanie's father, and mayor of Pompomville, he thinks everything is under control because he's running the show. Considers himself a real technological turning point and can't believe that the times have changed without consulting him. Will step on blue suede shoes...

Timothy Tremblay Fine strapping lad. Tangled up in his britches. About as sensitive as his engine. Has been in love with his modified V-8 for the past few years. Revs up for Bibi.

Mariette Malo Aerobic mother. A real woman and proud of it. Has always supported her husband, Maurice. Watch out! She's got a tigress in her tank!

Pheda Simard Seventy-five years worth of anarchy and this is only the beginning. Travels faster than bad news! Lucid, likeable and pretty "stylish" for her age. She's been wearing red shoes for years.

Jeannine Waitress by profession. Navigates in draft beer like a fish in water. Philosophical, she has a horsey, easy laugh. Likes her customers, her job and her boss, but...*don't step on her blue suede shoes*...

Stephanie Teenager, quick on her feet, doesn't pull any punches. Offstage voice.

SET

Act One, three locations: the kitchen in Mariette and Maurice Malo's house; the mayor's tavern "The Male Sin-Drome": Fine Food, Ladies Welcome; and "Miss Autobody", the local garage, (hence the title!). Act Two, the theatre becomes the chic cabaret, "The Sex Complex".

MUSIC

One or two synthesizers or an electric keyboard and/or anything you can get your hands on. Our piano player also played the accordion! The show was constantly punctuated by sound effects such as zip, zoom, crash, boom, bang, just like in a cartoon or an opera where the music reinforces, underlines or even announces the action and/or the text. If you have a synthesizer, rack your brains to "create" sounds other than the usual atmosphere music — it's worth the trouble!

ACTING

Les Folles Alliées strongly recommend that the play be performed by women only. The caricature is all the more effective. It can be interesting to have the action take place throughout the theatre, but if that is impossible, all four locations can easily be set up on a proscenium stage. You can also perform Miss Autobody in the privacy of your own home.

COSTUMES

For the Pink Brigade we chose white overalls which we silk-screened ourselves! You can wear something else under them and dress up over them. The mayor and mayoress are chic, as is befitting a mayor and mayoress. Pheda is old-fashioned with a modern touch. Jeannine is a sexy barmaid; she wears a leatherette skirt in Act One and a costume of the "tropical fish" ilk in the cabaret, Act Two. Timothy is in his car throughout the show. His car is his costume, his second skin. In our show, it was made of styrofoam with the customary horn and headlights. It's surprisingly effective!

READING INSTRUCTIONS

As with *Enfin Duchesses!*, also published by les Editions des Folles Alliées, we'd like to give you some friendly advice: read the script out loud, at the risk of looking crazy — it's much more fun that way!

'Kay, Bye!

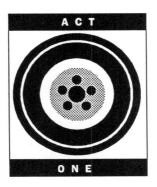

SCENE 1
At the Pink Brigade Headquarters

As the audience arrives, three members of the PINK BRIGADE mingle with the crowd. They are "secret agents."

Suspense music.

Two of the agents go onto the stage without seeing each other. Facing in opposite directions, they back up, from time to time executing a dance step (a routine where the feet tapdance and the arms perform the breast stroke) and saying "BRRR," the Pink Brigade password. They finally bump into each other and a phone rings. BARBARA takes a portable phone out of her pocket and BEATRICE takes the rest of the apparatus out of hers.

Barbara: Hello! Pink Brigade Headquarters, go ahead please ... Bonjour! l'Agence des Brigades roses, je vous écoute ... Pronto! La brigada rosa escouta ... Gutentag! Die Brigaden Rosen ist listening ... Buenos dias, las brigadas rosas escuchen ... Ah! It's you, Mrs. Poulin! Yes, Mrs. Poulin ... No, Mrs. Poulin ... I think so, Mrs. Poulin ... Okay, Mrs. Poulin ... Goodbye, Mrs. Poulin!

(She hangs the receiver up on BEATRICE'S phone.) That was Mrs. Poulin.[1]

Beatrice: *(relieved)* Ah! *(shouts)* Barbara Brigade! Last verification before annual vacation! *(BARBARA stands at attention. There is a change in tone.)* OK! The "Miss" contests?

Barbara: *(As if she had notepads all over her, she makes check marks on her hat, the lining of her coat, under her arm, on the sole of her shoe, etc.)* Check!

Beatrice: The sex shop on St. Joseph Street?

Barbara: Check!

Beatrice: Status of Women?

Barbara: Contacted.

Beatrice: Pierre Trudeau?

Barbara: *(looks at Beatrice, intrigued)* Re-elected?

Beatrice: The film reels?

Barbara: Check!

Beatrice: Pope John-Paul II?

Barbara: *(She makes a check mark on the hem of her coat she pulls through her legs.)* Check!

Beatrice: Okay!

Barbara: Beatrice Brigade! Last verification before annual vacation! The "Women Say No" stickers?

---

1 Mrs. Poulin really was les Folles Alliées' neighbour and she made a mean *tourtière* (a meatpie from the Lac St. Jean region).

Beatrice: *(makes no check mark)* Printed!

Barbara: *(intrigued)* La Vie en Rose?[1]

Beatrice: Subscriptions ordered!

Barbara: The billboards?

Beatrice: All sprayed!

Barbara: The guys across the street?

Beatrice: Forewarned.

Barbara: Mrs. Poulin's granddaughter's bicycle?

Beatrice: Mrs. Poulin's granddaughter's … oh, right! Repaired!

Barbara: Ah ha! Looks like we've hit vacation time! Right?

> *BEATRICE makes check marks all over her body, faster than the speed of light, while BARBARA isn't looking.*

Beatrice: Right?

Barbara: We're ready!

Beatrice: Ah! I've got my ready-to-travel outfit!

Barbara: Good, but we'll just make a list before we leave!

Together: *(Improvisation in the background while BRIGITTE, another Brigade, enters.)*

> *BRIGITTE, disguised as a newspaper, enters backwards. She bumps into the other two, starts in fear, recognizes her friends, smiles, and does the password.*

1 *La vie en rose* (feminist newsmagazine, published in Montreal from 1980-1987, R.I.P.)

Brigitte: BRRR! Hey! Girls! Can't we stop moving our headquarters around all the time? Keeping everything secret is great, but it seems to me we could let each other know! I had a terrible time finding us today! Good thing I ran into Mrs. Poulin! I don't know how she managed to recognize me.

Beatrice and Barbara: Are you ready?

All Three Together: *(Going-on-vacation improvisation in the background while another Brigade, BEVERLEY, enters.)*

> *BEVERLEY is dressed for both winter and summer at the same time, as in an overcoat and a wool cap, and a scuba diving mask.*

Beverley: *(In a hurry and frozen, she calls over her shoulder.)* Okay, Mrs. Poulin! Yes, Mrs. Poulin, don't worry. Oh, hi, girls! God, I was cold. I thought my brain was going to freeze waiting for the bus! *(The others look at each other knowingly.)* What's the date today?

The Others: *(pointing to the audience)* We're in the middle of the summer!

Beverley: God, I'm absentminded! Would you believe I've been freezing all day! *(The others tap their feet.)* Ummm, at the last meeting, I asked whether we could change the password. You know how it upsets me! *(The others indicate that it's out of the question. She does the password.)* BRRR! Are you ready?

All Together: BRRR! We're ready!

> *They all exit, except for BRIGITTE.*

Brigitte: Who's in charge of the answering machine?

> *They all return.*

Beatrice: Ach! *(Abbreviation of Aw hhheck or Aw hhhell!)* All right, I'll leave the message. *(MUSIC: Introduction to "Ze Girls On Vacation.")*

The Pink Brigades are currently away on vacation. At the sound of the BRRR, please leave a message!

All Together: BRRR!

Needless to say, all the songs are punctuated by choreography ("prretty chorreographies," as John Paul II would say). In the following song, the PINK BRIGADES imitate a trip by bus, arrival at the beach, a picnic, a tanning session, and some "wild" swimming. All while singing:

Ze Girls On Vacation[1]

Chorus: *(all)*

Ze girls on vacation
C'est si bon
Ze girls on vacation
C'est si bon

Just lie on the sand
Surrender to the sea
Hey girls, c'est si bon!

Beatrice:
Just lying there for hours and hours
With the sun on your skin
And you tell yourself lazily
Oh yes, this is my body

Chorus: Ze girls …

Brigitte:
Let your thoughts soar, fly like frisbees
In the clear blue sky
And you tell yourself gently
Oh yes, this is my body

1 The original version is available on 45 rpm.

Chorus: Ze girls ...

Beverley:
Your bottle of champagne
Buried in the sand
And you tell yourself gaily
This is my body

Chorus: Ze girls ...

Barbara:
Your toes in the water, your heart on ice,
You greet a passing fly
And you tell yourself happily
Oh yes, this is my body.

Chorus: Ze girls ...

Finale:
Beverley: Si bon, si bon, si bon
All Together: Tayadada ...

Telephone: DRRRING!

> *The song is interrupted by the phone. They all freeze, then turn slowly towards BEATRICE. They tap their temples, as in: "Are you crazy, or what?"*

Barbara: Didn't you set it to "Answer"?

Beatrice: Achh!

Brigitte: Hello!? La brigada escouten, habla english, sprechen sie Portugal? Going on vacaciones, pronto!

Bibi: *(off)* OK! OK! I know the message by heart, Brigitte, it's Bibi!

> *They all turn toward BRIGITTE.*

Brigitte: Ah, it's the Bibi Brigade! *(to BIBI)* But who gave you our new number? We just had it changed!

Bibi: *(off)* Well, I called Mrs. —

All Together: Ahh!

Bibi: *(off)* Phew! You haven't left yet. That's great because I wanted to invite you all to come visit me in Pompomville!

Brigitte: Pompomville?

Bibi's Voice: That's right! It's wonderful, it's beautiful, it's on the ocean, it's got everything: canoeing, windsurfing, ice cream, French-fry stands and my garage!

Brigitte: Your garage?!

Bibi's Voice: Right again! I just bought myself a garage and I thought you could all come and help me out during your vacation. *(MUSIC indicating general consternation among the BRIGADES.)* So that's how it is, now that I'm the mission!

Brigitte: Well … why not. We accept. We'll all be there!

Bibi's Voice: Do you know where Pompomville is?

Beatrice: *(wakes up)* Pompomville! Mrs. Poulin used to have a cottage near there. Geographically speaking, in Pompomville one finds all the elements that lead to the formation of a microclimate … *(No one is listening as she rattles on.)*

Brigitte: OK! Bibi, I don't think we'll have any trouble finding it. One of us here seems to know how to get there. Bye!

They all exit, except for BEATRICE, who carries on.

Beatrice: It's Quebec's finest resort town, a real St. Tropez!

Beverley: *(returns)* Beatrice! C'mon, don't worry, we'll take care of the answering machine! *(three broad winks)*

Beatrice: Achh! Sorry 'bout that, I got a bit … *(she is looking for something)* … the keys to the van … *(desperate)* … hey, girls!

She runs offstage.

SCENE 2
At the Garage

"Miss Autobody" song.

For this song, the choreography is as close to the "musical revue" style as possible. The BRIGADES greet BIBI with kisses all around. They start to clean up the garage, throwing out the girlie magazines and calendars, cleaning, decorating, etc. All of this while singing:

Miss Autobody

Bibi:
Time to work
Get to work
Away with the spider webs
And we'll make the whole place sparkle
And we'll make the whole place shine
Then dear garage
What are we going to call you?

> *The others enter, singing in a whisper: "Time to work, get to work," and take BIBI by surprise.*

Bibi: No!

Everyone: Yes!

All Together:
Away with the spiderwebs
And we'll make the whole place sparkle
And we'll make the whole place shine
Then dear garage
What are we going to call you?

Sweep away the tried untrue
To hell with these magazines

Oooh oooh oooh ahhh!
Sweep away the traditions
To hell with the old decor
Oooh oooh oooh ahhh!

Get to work
Get to work
We're not afraid of grease
Or dirtying our hands
Motor oil smells like Christmas
But dear garage
What are we going to call you?

Sweep away the tried untrue
To hell with these magazines
Sweep away the traditions
To hell with the old decor
Oooh oooh oooh ahhh!

All ready
All ready
Ready for your baptism
Your name will be original
Both feminine and commercial
Dear ... Miss ... Autobody
Dear, dear ... Miss ... Miss ... Autobody

> *Blackout on stage. The words "Miss Autobody" appear on the garage.*

Bibi: *(unrolling a long list)* I prepared a little list of chores we could divide up between us.

Beverley: Hey, I think it's beachtime now.

Beatrice: Follow me, I know where it is. Mrs. Poulin used to have a cottage near here ...

Barbara: I'm going to do a bit of advertising for you around town.

Miss Autobody

*They exit faster than the speed of light. Except for BRIGITTE,
who walks off slowly.*

Brigitte: And I'm going to check out the French-fry Stand. It's been a
long time since I've had some real French fries with ketchup and
mayonnaise … *(BIBI blocks her way.)* Oh well, what the heck, I guess
I'll stay here and help you.

*They study the list of chores together. BRIGITTE gives all sorts
of advice and sits down on the front steps of the garage while BIBI
tackles the cleanup alone.*

SCENE 3
At "The Male Sin-Drome"

Barbara: I'll just leave this on the counter for you.

Jeannine: Fine, I'll take care of it.

BARBARA turns to leave the bar-restaurant while still talking to JEANNINE. She bumps into MAURICE, the mayor, and steps on his foot. MAURICE is still carrying his attaché case.

Maurice: I hope the little lady didn't hurt herself?

Barbara: She didn't! But if you've got any bumps or scrapes, come see us at "Miss Autobody!"

MAURICE and BARBARA exchange polite greetings and BARBARA exits.

Maurice: Owwww! What did *she* want?

Jeannine: *(bending over to examine MAURICE's foot)* She came to drop off a flier for the garage.

Maurice: *(with a penetrating stare)* Hey! They're looking good this morning, your … sweater!

Jeannine: *(slaps his foot)* You're raring to go bright and early this morning, Maurice. Something feeling too big for your britches already? *(She laughs.)*

Maurice: Whoa, Jeannine. I've got work to do. I have a few little things to screen.

MAURICE turns on a TV set using a remote control.

Jeannine: *(opening MAURICE's briefcase)* Not such little things from what I can see. "Perverse Passion," "Memoirs of a Pair of Lace Panties," "Hitchhiking Prey," "Rape in the Tropics."[1]

Maurice: They're not for here, Jeannine. They're for Saturday night, for the opening of my new bar, "The Sex Complex."

Jeannine: Thank God. 'Cause even the so-called "soft-core" items you show here get the customers pretty worked up. If you started showing those here, the guys'd go right over the top. I'd have to keep a gun under the bar, like in a saloon. *(She points a bottle at MAURICE.)* Hands up! You all pull up your pants and put away your pistols, or Little Red Riding Hood is gonna make you all look like swiss cheese! *(She laughs.)*

Maurice: *(his eyes rivetted to the screen)* They're made to get you all worked up, and they do just that.

Jeannine: Well, I've seen so many, I'm so worked up, I cream my pants so bad I have to keep a mop behind the bar! *(She guffaws.)*

Maurice: Don't tell me you've started to turn frigid.

Jeannine: Ah! That must be what's wrong with me! Every since you brought that thing in here, all the customers think they're Superman. I'm scared. *(She climbs up onto the bar and continues in a tiny voice.)* Help! Help! Who's going to show me my real self? Help, I beg of you, help! *(The mop stick appears between her legs.)*

Maurice: God, you're crazy. Are you about to lose what's left of your senses? Take it easy, try putting yourself on cruise control.

Jeannine: Cruise-control, you kidding me? There's no stopping me, Maurice. Full speed ahead, flat out. I want a man. Right away! I need a man. Can't get enough. One ... *(She chooses one, then several men from the audience.)* ... two ... three ... ten. ... baby, baby, baby ... A whole army. *(She picks up a spray bottle.)* I'm burning with desire. All the firemen in the country couldn't put out the fire burning here inside

---

1 For current titles, consult your local video club catalogue.

me. *(She aims the spray bottle between her legs and laughs again.)* Hello, Nicole! I saw such a great porno movie, you gotta see it. The story is so beautiful, I was crying at the end!

Maurice: *(staring at the screen)* Okay, okay, maybe you need a change. Why don't you try watching some videoclips.

Jeannine: Great idea, a real change. *(She sings.)* Thriller, thriller … Haaaaaa *(She screams.)*[1]

Maurice: *(annoyed, distracted)* OK, OK, peace in our time, Jeannine, peace in our time, all right?

Jeannine: Right, Momo, peace in our time. *(As she turns to go back behind the bar, she growls at MAURICE like a cat in heat.)*

> TIMOTHY *enters the bar-restaurant, complete with his beautiful car. He is very noisy and upset.*

Timothy: *(out of breath)* The ga … the ga … the gaga … the garage!

Jeannine: What's wrong with the garage, Timothy?

Timothy: There are these chick … chick …

Maurice: *(surprised)* There are chickens in the garage?

Timothy: No … these chicks have taken over the garage!

Maurice and Jeannine: *(relieved)* Ah!

Timothy: You mean you don't care that Marcel sold his garage to a bunch of girls?

Jeannine: Welcome to equal opportunity, Tim.

Maurice: Give him a beer, Jeannine, that'll calm him down. *(in a*

---

1 Or any other videoclip where a girl gets pushed around. (Note from Jeannine.)

municipal tone of voice) C'mon, Tim, you know there's no future for a town where businesses close down. *(looking at the screen)* Wow, Tim, is she your size?

Timothy: *(surprised by the question)* Oh, the girl! But, as Mayor, Mr. Malo —

Maurice: Call me Maurice. Come have a seat, my boy.

Timothy: If some girl bought the garage … who's going to repair our cars? *(He takes a sip of his beer and calms down as he watches the video.)* Oh well, I'm getting all worked up for nothing. *(He settles into his car accompanied by an electronic "zwip zwozzzz" sound effect which is heard each time he sits back.)* Her boyfriend or her husband will show up and he'll turn out to be the mechanic.

Maurice: No, Tim. She must've taken one of those non-traditional courses. *(looking at the screen)* Wow! He sure took care of her!

MAURICE and TIMOTHY stare at the TV screen.

Jeannine: C'mon, you guys. Times have changed. We're more than just waitresses at the banquet of life. Those days are gone forever, boys.

Maurice: Listen, Tim, women's lib is no big deal. It's been around for years now. 'Bout time you caught up.

Timothy: Sure, sure, but a woman fiddling around with my carburetor … Whoa! I'm willing to flip a lot of switches, but … this car is … *(MUSIC from the film "Love Story")* … it's my life, Maurice. Every Saturday night, I wash her, I polish her. I always save the best pieces for her. I've sacrificed a lot for her.

> *MUSIC from the Serge Gainsbourg song "Je t'aime, moi non plus,"*[1] *while TIMOTHY, let's call a spade a spade, humps his car. He pants.*

1 The most famous (and provocative) French love song of the 1970s.

JOAN TREMBLAY

"Times have changed. We're more than just waitresses at the banquet of life. Those days are gone forever, boys."

Timothy: Last winter, I worked overtime to buy her those furry slipcovers. She's got the best body around! *(He lights up a cigarette, "animal [sic] triste," as in post-coital depression.)* But this car, Maurice, she's so sensitive, so delicate. Every summer, I take her to the States so she can see the ocean. I'm the only one who really understands her. The only one who ever lays a hand on her. The only other person I ever trusted was Marcel. *(panic)* I knew he respected her. But those girls — they might mess around inside her with ... with ... with knitting needles![1] Never, Maurice. Over my dead body!

Maurice: *(looking at the screen)* It's true, some women go a bit too far!

Jeannine: Sometimes the stuff you have to listen to makes you wish you were deaf! A woman mechanic never killed a man!

> *JEANNINE goes into the audience to clear the tables. Both men look at her as if to say: "You making fun of us?"*

Maurice: What do you expect me to do about it? I already issued the permit, she's legal.

Timothy: Legal maybe, but not equal. She's not Marcel's equal, I can tell you that. And now what am I gonna do? I got some little thing knocking around in my engine.

Jeannine: Well, why don'tcha go to the garage and show her your little thing! *(She laughs.)* If she's seen that kind of thing before, she'll fix it up for you. Don't turn you nose up at a meal before you've tasted it. *(She laughs again.)*

Maurice: You just gave me a great idea, Jeannine. Treat yourself to a beer! Get ready, Tim. Let's go over to the garage and meet that little girl. We'll put her to the test.

Jeannine: Now what are you up to, Maurice Malo?

Maurice: Don't worry about a thing, Jeannine. First of all, this is

---

1 Why do we usually mess around with knitting needles? Owch!

between men, and besides, you know me well enough to know I wouldn't harm a little girl. C'mon, Tim, it'll be good for a laugh. You going to give me a lift?

MAURICE and TIMOTHY exit.

Jeannine: Now I can give my eyes a break! *(She turns the TV off.)* Have to protect my eyes from occupational hazards! *(She laughs.)*

SCENE 4
The Kitchen
(at home with the mayor's wife)

At first Mrs. Malo (MARIETTE) appears with her back to us as the previous scene "fades out." On her head she is wearing a bowl with exotic fruit hanging from it. Holding a mixing bowl, she starts moving to the music of "La Cucaracha." The atmosphere is aerobic.

Mariette: *(singing)* She was a nice girl, a proper girl, BUT, one of the rovin' kind!

Stephanie's Voice: Mommy, where's my hockey sweater?

MARIETTE continues singing and counts: one, two, three, as she does her exercises.

Stephanie's Voice: Mom ... Mom ... Mommy!!

Mariette: Stephanie, don't tell me that at your age you can't stick your head in the dryer!

Stephanie's Voice: Found it! *(dull thump)* Owch! Sh ...

Mariette: Stephanie!

Stephanie's Voice: ... oot. Who's coming to pick me up at the rink after practice?

Mariette: Don't you worry, sweetie, your father or I will. Or I'll send Timothy. Anyway, someone will be there. Score lots of goals now, mommy's proud of you!

Stephanie's Voice: If it's gonna be Timothy, forget it. I'd rather walk home.

Mariette: What have you got against Timothy?

Stephanie's Voice: Aw, he always tells these dumb jokes and he bothers me. Bye! I'm late.

Mariette: Don't slam the door!

Slam! Followed by a second slam.

Mariette: Steph … *(PHEDA enters.)* Oh, it's you, Mrs. Simard!

Pheda: Hello, my dear. I've finished your quilt for you, look. Pretty nice, eh?

Mariette: Ah … you did it. Stephanie's going to be happy!

Pheda: I guess so, girl! I figured she likes hockey so much … what do you think? *(On one side of the quilt, she shows her the Quebec City Nordiques' insignia.)* And if she changes her mind as she gets older, well … *(On the other side is the Montreal Canadiens' insignia.[1])*

Mariette: It must've taken you days! *(She passes her bowl to PHEDA and takes the quilt.)*

Pheda: *(worried)* Princess! Princess!

Mariette: Don't tell me you left her outside?

Pheda: I guess she got caught in the door or in the stairway, or something.

Mariette: Stay right there. I'll go get her for you.

Pheda: *(alone on stage)* What was she up to, anyway? *(She tastes the salad dressing.)* Not enough Dungeon mustard!

---

1 Substitute your favourite rival hockey teams. You'll get cheers and boos from both sides.

"I've finished your quilt for you, look. Pretty nice, eh?"

Mariette: Here's her ladyship! *(She brings in a rocking chair!)*

Pheda: *(happy to see her chair)* Ah! Pretty Princess. *(She sits down.)* Listen, Mariette, you'll never guess where I've just been!

Mariette: Never, Pheda.

Pheda: *(talks a blue streak and rocks her chair a blue streak)* Well, you know me, eh? I go for my walks around town, I take lots of walks, my doctor, he told me: "It's good for your legs, Mrs. Simard, and it's good for your arthritis on top of that." So, come rain or shine, I go for my walks around town. *(pauses and begins again more slowly)* And today, I stopped by the garage!

Mariette: *(busy examining the quilt)* Uh huh.

Pheda: *(talking a blue streak while rocking her chair a blue ...)* Well, some people claim that a woman my age has no business going to make a scene at the garage, but I didn't go to make a scene, I just went to see for myself, to see for myself, that's all. I like poking my nose into everything that goes on in town. I always liked to keep up with the times and the changes. *(slowly)* The other day, I noticed there was just one girl at the garage, and I let it be. But then, when I saw there was a whole gang of young girls over there, I figured it was about time someone welcomed them to town.

Mariette: *(distractedly)* Uh huh.

Pheda: *(at breakneck speed)* Besides, if anyone in town cares about good manners, it's me. Ah, manners, etiquette, tradition, there's a lot to be said for it, my dear. Seems to me it's just natural, you greet people when they arrive, you say goodbye when they leave. Pompomville is going to stay a polite town if I have anything to say about it. In spite of my age, I always try to practice good manners. I always did like good manners! *(slowly)* Well, I know that as the mayor's wife, you're really busy, so I said to myself: "Pheda, as the oldest resident of Pompomville, it's your duty!"

Mariette: Uh huh. So … would you like a cup of coffee, Pheda?

Pheda: No thanks! *(a blue streak)* Don't want to impose, my dear. I just stopped in on my way by. *(She stops short and looks at MARIETTE, who doesn't say a thing.)* Well, if you insist, it's my treat! *(Not knowing what to do with the bowl with the salad dressing, she puts it on her head upside down. Then she takes a thermos out of the backpack hanging on the rocker.)* You take one sugar and eight milks, right?

Mariette: Right.

Pheda: Well, that's how I made it, I remembered, by gosh, I remembered! *(sits back down and puts the bowl back on her knees)* So you should've seen them over at the garage. Singing away, cleaning away. A real beehive. If you ask me, they're going to liven things up around here! Busy, busy, busy!

  They toast.

Mariette: Hmmm, good coffee, Pheda. You're right, we needed some new faces around town. But girls running a garage — I know a few people who are going to blow their gaskets!

Pheda: Their engines are going to overheat!

  They laugh and laugh and laugh.

Pheda: Listen, Mariette, it's probably none of my business, but … *(She puts the bowl on the floor.)*

Mariette: But, what, Pheda? *(She puts down the quilt.)*

Pheda: Maurice's new "complex" — isn't it supposed to open on Saturday night? *(She kicks aside the bowl.)*

Mariette: Don't tell me you're going to start in on that again, Pheda. Seems to me we could find something else to talk about. You've been going on about that for the last three months. *(She kicks aside the quilt.*

Each kick is accompanied by a sound effect on the keyboard.)

Pheda: But you don't seem to be aware of what's happening, Mariette Malo!

Mariette: *(another kick)* What do you mean, "aware," Pheda Simard! Are you aware of Pompomville's economic boom?

Pheda: Only thing I see booming is bare bums!

They both cross their knees and raise their teacups.

Mariette: *(She gestures with her cup.)* We're well known now, people come here to have fun and spend their money.

Pheda: *(Her cup is dancing now too.)* Have you seen those movies they're showing over at The Male Sin-Drome?

Mariette: Our town's name is on the highway signs now.

Pheda: It all started with those magazine racks at the newsstand and the grocery store, then at the garage.

Mariette: "Have to follow the trends, if you want to keep people happy," as Maurice always says.

Pheda: But naked girls all over the place? Everywhere! Lying around, tied up, inside out, upside down!

Mariette: We used to have pedalboats, now we have windsurfing!

Pheda: And they're watching those videos in every house in town.

Mariette: And now, we're going to have a cabaret!

Pheda: If this stuff was really fun, I'd laugh along with the best of them.

Together: Anyway ...

Pheda: Anyway ... *(She resumes talking a blue ...)* I can tell you a thing or two about conversations like this, cause at my age, this isn't the first one I've had! And I know exactly what's going to happen. *(louder)* I walk in here with my ideas, you stick to your ideas, and we go 'round in circles, dear girl, you hear me? 'Round in circles!

> *She offers MARIETTE another cup of coffee. MARIETTE refuses. PHEDA pours the rest of her cup back into the thermos, while muttering away.*

Pheda: Look at us. And I thought we could have a nice talk between friends. I even brought along some cookies, but you're not going to get any!

Mariette: Listen, Pheda! Times have changed! Things aren't the same anymore.

Pheda: *(angry)* Good thing I heard that at my age and in my lifetime, cause in the next life nobody will believe me. If there is one ...

Mariette: One what?

Pheda: A next life.

Mariette: *(impatient but not angry)* Listen, Pheda, please, just listen to me! You have to accept progress. People are more open-minded now.

Pheda: Just because you have the TV on all day doesn't mean your mind is more open!

Mariette: I've watched some of those videos and they're no big deal! They help men relieve their tensions, and when they're watching those films, they're not hurting anyone. It's like a release for them.

Pheda: *(sighs, brings her hand to her chest, then takes MARIETTE's hand and pats it)* When you see a cheese ad, you feel like eating cheese, right? When you see a beer ad, you feel like having a beer, right? Well, just what do you think those videos release, eh, Mariette? And who bears the brunt of their release, eh?

Mariette: *(She has run out of answers.)* Well, that's just the way men are, Pheda!

Pheda: Well, if I was a man and they told me "that's just the way men are," I'd be pretty insulted, believe you me! You sound like old Father Charette. He always used to tell me, "You have to do your duty, Mrs. Simard, that's just the way men are." Well, my dear, I finally earned some respect, and after I had my eighth child, I kicked Father Charette out of the house.

Mariette: What does Father Charette have to do with this? Those old taboos are gone now.

The MUSIC begins.

Pheda: Those old taboos ... Those old taboos ... Did you hear that, Princess?

The choreography for this song is relatively simple, given PHEDA's respectable age. Her interpretation is pure "hoedown" style. She mimes the words of the song and walks back and forth, with the occasional quick dance step thrown in for good measure. Three Lipton soup packages form a chorus in the background!

Pheda's Song

Chorus:

Those old taboos (bis)
Did you hear that, Princess (bis)
In my days
It was close your eyes
And grit your teeth
But today
It's open your legs
Duck for the oyster, do-si-do!

Just who
Got to decide
That what
For you and for me was
Just bang, bang, bang
Was fun and games?

Chorus: Those old taboos ...

In my days
The sermons said
That we were just
Sinful temptation
And today
We lie naked
On stands and shelves
It's just more
Of the same damn story

Just who
Got to decide
That what
For me and for you
Was just boom, boom, boom
Was better and new?

Chorus: Those old taboos ...

In my days
Our lives were hell on earth
Then they kept our asses
Tied to our stoves
But today
They have us down on all fours
And keep us tied up
In their tits and ass films

To MARIETTE, whom she invites to join her in a square dance.[1]

1 Square dance, set dance, who knows, that was before our time! (Note from the Lipton Soup packages.)

Just when
Are we gonna
Decide what
Really makes me and you
Most unhappy, unhappy
And afraid, afraid too?

Chorus: Those old taboos ...

In my days
I always felt like
A cow
Good for breeding
And today
I feel like
A fat pig
On a meat rack

If times have really changed
Tell me why you and I
Should turn on the TV
And sit there and see
More handsome roosters
Chase the poor hens
And strut and crow?

Pheda: *(spoken)* Can you please tell me why, Mariette Malo? You give them your hand, they break your leg! Princess! Princess, come here, Girl!

> *PHEDA exits ... followed by her rocking chair!*

> *MARIETTE, alone on stage, gathers up her salad dressing bowl and the quilt. She sings, at first to herself, then more and more to the audience.*

> *Four men wearing fedoras join her for the next song.*

"Just when / Are we gonna / Decide what / Really makes me and you / Most unhappy, unhappy / And afraid, afraid too?"

Boys Will Be Boys

Now they do the dishes
And they listen to our wishes
They decorate their virile chests
With gold chains and silver crests

> *One man comes forward and looks her over from head to toe, then
> goes back to stand with the others.*

But there's always the one
In the street
Who gives you one of those looks
One of those looks that leave no doubt
Careful, watch out!
Don't forget, boys will be boys

> *The men lift her onto their shoulders, carry her in their arms, then
> put her down.*

They can reach the highest shelf
They carry bags and open doors
They call for an end to all wars
They sleep in your arms, innocence itself

> *One of the men comes closer, glances furtively to his left, to his
> right, then bends her over in two and leaves. She straightens up
> on her own.*

But there's always the one
In the news
An act that brought fear and pain
The story which leaves no doubt
Careful, watch out
Don't forget, boys will be boys
Their beards are so silky
And their smiles so fine
We cavort in their arms
Like a cat in the sunshine

She dances with a partner who grabs her bum.

But there's always the one
In a club
Who gives you a look so vile
A smile that leaves no doubt
Careful, watch out
Don't forget, boys will be boys
They laugh like sails in the wind
Children want them to wrestle and play
They put their ear to our bellies
Tender as doves at the break of day

*The men stamp their heels flamenco style and turn their backs to
her.*

But there's always one
Some day some night
Who claims he's got a right
In words that leave no doubt
Careful, watch out
Don't forget, boys will be boys

*One man remains with her briefly, then exits before the end of the
song.*

If we were alone just us two
We'd work it out, talk it through
Love can make it confusing
Sometimes you feel like refusing
To say to another
See that man, he's my lover.

Blackout on stage. Silence.

SCENE 5
The Test

TIMOTHY and MAURICE arrive at the garage. They pull up noisily and come to an abrupt stop.

Maurice: Attaboy! Quite the cowboy!

Timothy: Were you scared, Mo?

Maurice: Scared, no. It's just that I know you've got some little thing knocking around in your engine.

Timothy: Now it's more than some little thing. You sure it was a good idea connecting the horn to the hood, the radio to the heater, and the wipers to the lighter?

Maurice: You better believe it. It's gonna be a riot. *(The horn honks.)* She won't even notice. *(in his election campaign tone of voice)* They can't take a few night courses and make us believe that any fool can learn to fix an engine.

Brigitte: Hello!

Maurice: Hmmmm!

Timothy: Let me introduce the mayor of Pompomville.

Brigitte: My pleasure. Should I fill her up?

Timothy: No, it's more serious than that.

Brigitte: What's the matter? Ooops! Wait a minute, don't tell me. Just looking at you I can tell you've got some little thing knocking around in your engine.

Timothy: That's right. But there's something else wrong too, and I'd like you to take a look at it.

Brigitte: Oh, not me, I don't know a thing about mechanics. No, I'm more of a physiognomist. You see, I'm interested in the psychology of cars. And more specifically, the psychology of drivers. A car's life history often reflects the life history of its owner. Let me give you an example. Some people pull up here and you can see at a glance that their batteries are run down. Others pull up so tense, clutching the steering wheel like their life depended on it. It's a dead giveaway. Their brakes are usually worn to shreds.

Maurice: *(seeing that TIMOTHY is horrified)* Why are you looking so amazed? Don't have to be Einstein to figure that out.

Brigitte: Well, enough of this chewing the fat, passing the time of day, as they say. Don't worry, I'll go get the real mechanic for you.

> *She concentrates and presses her fingertips to her temples. We hear the familiar "ding dong" of gas stations. BIBI appears with her knitting; TIMOTHY flips his lid.*

Timothy: *(pointing to the knitting needles)* I'm never gonna let you fiddle around inside my car with those.

> *MUSIC: The theme from "Love Story." It's love at first sight.*

Bibi: *(smitten)* What wrong with him? Has he got some little thing knocking around in his engine? *(She hands her knitting to BRIGITTE.)*

Maurice: This morning my friend Timmy was telling me about his car trouble. I said to him: "Why don't you go see the girls at the garage. You have to support the town's economy. I issued their permits, don't treat them like hermits."

Bibi: Very kind of you, Mayor Malo.

Maurice: *(pleased)* That's the way things are around here. A healthy mayor in a healthy town.

Bibi: No need to panic, here's the lady mechanic. Let Bibi look and see what your car's trouble can be.[1]

Timothy: Let me show you how it opens.

Bibi: I assume it's here? *(The horn honks.)* Hey, that's strange!

Timothy: I told you there was something wrong. This is no motorbike. Bet you've never seen such a big one, eh?

Bibi: *(her head under the hood of the car)* Gotta hand it to you, it's a beauty and it's a big one alright. But I'd like to know who had the bright idea of connecting the horn to the hood, the radio to the heater and the wipers to the lighter?

Maurice: Hmmmm! If you don't mind, I'd like to inspect the premises. As chief of the volunteer firemen, I have to make sure everything meets the regulations.

BIBI: Brigitte, could you show the mayor around?

Brigitte: My pleasure.

> BRIGITTE and MAURICE disappear. BIBI puts her head back under the hood.

Bibi: Wow! A modified V-8! Two carburetors and an overhead camshaft. Pretty clever. That must give you one helluva kick.

Timothy: Every so often, some wise guy pulls up beside me looking for trouble. But I just rev her up a bit and he gets the picture right away.

Bibi: You must've spent quite a few weekends on her.

Timothy: Every Saturday with Marcel. When I bought her, she wasn't anything like this.

---

1 Did you notice how it's funnier when you read it out loud?

"Bet you've never seen such a big one, eh?"

Fade out. BRIGITTE and MAURICE reappear inspecting the garage. Semi-darkness. Fortunately, MAURICE has a flashlight.

Maurice: Tell me, Miss Brigitte?

Brigitte: Yes?

Maurice: Are you here as Miss Bibi's associate?

Brigitte: Yes, that's right, you could call us associates.

Maurice: Looks like you cleaned the place up. Guess you didn't like Marcel's decorations? Anyway, I think it's much nicer now that you've taken over.

Brigitte: Would you like to see the emergency exit? It's over here.

Maurice: Don't you worry, we'll check it all out, young lady.

Brigitte: I'm sure you will, "young" man. Ha ha ha!

Maurice: That's one fine emergency exit, absolutely legal. But I'm not so sure I'd want to escape if I were caught inside here all alone with you, young lady. *(He thinks he's funny.)*

Brigitte: You might be surprised … young man! Ha ha ha! *(She thinks she's even funnier.)*

Maurice: Would you mind moving your … getting your … uh … *(She backs away, chest first.)* Thanks! You threw out those oil drums, how did you manage? They were really dirty and heavy, and they smelled something awful. It's a pity messing up your pretty little hands like that!

Brigitte: Would you like to see the washrooms? We cleaned them up. They were really dirty and they smelled something awful too.

Maurice: What do you expect? Marcel was a real mechanic. He was better with a screwdriver than with a mop. Miss Brigitte? I've got a little proposition for you.

Brigitte: *(interested)* I'm listening.

> *Fade out. TIMOTHY's song. Choreography: porno magazines manipulated by the PINK BRIGADES. MAURICE quickly becomes a Pink Brigade for the occasion.*

Which End Is Up?

The corner store is where us boys
Learned about love's secret joys
The first women to give us that feeling
Were naked, spread apart or kneeling
In the centerfolds

The movie theatre is where us boys
Got to spy on love's secret joys
The first women to nail us to our chair
Were naked, smiling, just lying there
On the silver screen

What can you say to a woman like that
Who talks about batteries and antifreeze
What can you say to a woman like that
Who knows your car like her ABCs
Eh! Tell me please *(repeat three times)*
Which end is up

Me and the boys, we always said
The women we love are gonna cry for joy in bed
Me and the boys, we always swore
The women we love would shout: Give me more, more!

But what can you say to a woman like that
Who talks about spark plugs and antifreeze
What can you say to a woman like that
Who knows your car like her ABCs

"The first women to nail us to our chair / Were naked, smiling, just lying there / On the silver screen ..."

Eh! Tell me please *(repeat three times)*
Which end is up

> *All the BRIGADES exit, except for BIBI, who remains on stage with TIMOTHY.*

Bibi: *(bangs her head as she straightens up)* Owww!

Timothy: Being a mechanic is tough!

Bibi: Good. I got it all sorted out, everything's working fine now. Could you start the car and back up a bit? OK ... OK. ... fine. Now, forward ... Whoa! I've fixed all the connections. It was dangerous, the engine could've caught on fire. Unless it was supposed to be some kind of joke. But if it was a joke, it wasn't such a smart idea. It almost burned out your alternator.

Timothy: What!

Bibi: Oh, I almost forgot. Should we take a look at that little thing of yours?

Timothy: *(embarrassed)* My little what?

Bibi: The little valve you say is knocking around in your engine.

Timothy: Oh, right.

> *Back to BRIGITTE and MAURICE, who are somewhere else inside the garage.*

Maurice: Did we really have to go through the attic?[1]

Bibi: You're the fireman.

Maurice: Miss Brigitte, let's forget that you're a woman and talk business.

---

1 Or, if you prefer, "through the cellar." Find a space you haven't used yet!

Brigitte: Sure, you just forget that you're a man, and I'll listen to you. Ha ha ha!

Maurice: I like it, I like it. You've got guts. We're gonna get along fine. Marcel was a nice guy, but he didn't keep up with the times. I'm a man of the future, and *you, (staring at her breasts)* well, you have a great future ahead of you. A garage offers an important service to the community, but a man can't necessarily make a living off it. Have you ever thought about ... about opening a little "convenience" stand right next to the garage? You could sell beer, cheese, and a few little videos ...

Brigitte: A few little what?

Maurice: We're both adults, right? Just between you and me, for thousands of years now, the bare essentials of leisure have been alcohol and sex. I'm proposing a partnership. You open the convenience store, I advance the money and the videos. Here's the catalogue. And we'll share the profits.

BRIGITTE leafs through the catalogue and seems surprised.

Brigitte: What kind of items would you like us to rent?

MAURICE takes some samples out of his briefcase.

Maurice: Well, I've got a bit of everything — family entertainment, rock music — but the big sellers, the most profitable stuff, is the erotic line.

Brigitte: *(interested)* Ah! Are you the distributor for this around here?

Maurice: That's right. And believe me, I had a hard time setting the business up. People are so conservative! But it broke my heart seeing them sneak through the streets on their way to those cheap movie theatres — that cost a fortune to boot. Videos are something else. They're affordable, and that makes them more democratic. You can watch them all comfy in a nice, clean living room. Even the intellectuals like them 'cause what they do at home is nobody's business!

Brigitte: You know, I'm not at all interested.

Maurice: We're in the middle of an economic crisis. And you're refusing big money. Think twice, before you throw the baby out with the bath water. I might've had another proposition, but I'm just wasting my time. I'm going to speak to the real owner.

Brigitte: Ha ha!

Blackout on the two of them.

Bibi: Anyway, Timothy, if you can come back on Saturday, we'll take another look at that. Quite the car you've got there, quite the car.

Timothy: Thanks a lot, Bibi. How much do I owe you?

Bibi: Nothing this time. I think someone played a trick on you.

Timothy: Well, in exchange, maybe I could invite you out on Saturday night. It's the inauguration of ...

MAURICE appears, with BRIGITTE following him at quite a distance. He gets lost in the audience.

Maurice: Miss Brigitte? Miss Brigitte? She ditched me, the little sonofagun! Ah! Miss Bibi! Miss Bibi, Saturday night I'm inaugurating my magnificent new exotic-erotic club. It's a major event in town and all the local businesses are participating by putting posters up in their windows ...

Bibi: No!

Maurice: ... and I thought I'd offer my guests, I know you'll be one of them ...

Bibi: No!

Maurice: ... a beautiful souvenir programme, printed on high-class glossy paper, with colour photos, the whole bit. And it only costs ... a hundred dollars!

Bibi: No!

Maurice: If I heard you right, you just said ... no?

Bibi and Brigitte: Yes!

Bibi: If I heard you right, Timothy, you wanted to invite me Saturday night ...

Timothy: No!

Maurice: C'mon, Timothy. We're going to be late. Bye now, Miss ... Autobody!

Timothy: Bye, Bibi. And thanks for the repair job.

MAURICE: Let's go, Timothy, move! Step on it!

They floor it.

Brigitte: Do you see what I see?

Bibi: Are you thinking what I'm thinking?

Bibi and Brigitte: BRRR!

SCENE 6
At the Male Sin-Drome Bar-Restaurant

Jeannine: *(singing as she puts away the empty bottles)* Don't you know, they're talkin' about a revolution ... Finally the tables are starting to turn, talkin' bout a revolution ... [1]

MAURICE and TIMOTHY enter the restaurant.

Maurice: Two beers, Jeannine, on the double.

Jeannine: Peace in our time, Maurice.

Maurice: *(mad)* Cat got your tongue? You didn't say a thing over at the garage. Sonny just sat there letting some girl fool around, fiddle around in his engine.

Timothy: *(madder)* But she's really good, Maurice. She knows cars! She's super terrific!

Maurice: Argh, and you're a lead-free sissy!

Timothy: Well, you're not so smart yourself. Your dumb idea almost burned out my alternator! A good thing she didn't charge me a penny.

Jeannine: That was nice of her. How come the two of you are so upset?

Maurice: *(appalled)* Can't you see them coming? I offered whatshername — Miss ... Bibi — a chance to go into business with me. She refused. Simple as that! Do you two kids realize what that means?

Jeannine: It just means that it's not their kind of business. And it means you've finally met your match! *(laughs)*

---

1 Or substitute any song from the top of the pops wherever you are.

Maurice: And what about you? It's not your kind of business, but you work here anyway!

Jeannine: That's different. *(pointing to the TV screen)* I had no choice when you decided to bring that in here. Well, listen, Maurice Malo, just because you've got a hair across your ass doesn't mean you can shit on me.

Maurice: I think I've seen enough of you for today, Jeannine. I think you've earned a nice long afternoon off. Bye!

Timothy: Don't worry about it, Jeannine. I owe you an afternoon. I'll replace you.

> *JEANNINE and MAURICE take each other on in a little tango that ends when JEANNINE plunks MAURICE down onto a chair and pulls his hat down over his eyes.*

Jeannine: See you later, guys. Try not to chomp on the bit now! *(She laughs.)*

> *JEANNINE exits through a door behind the bar.*

Maurice: *(Contained but on the verge of exploding, he raises his hat slowly and flies off the handle.)* How uptight can you get! Have to handle 'em with kid gloves. Like those two girls at the garage — Miss ...

Timothy: Bibi?

Maurice: I know her name for crying out loud! Go ahead, why don't you take sides with them too. Go ahead, tell me I'm macho.

> *From offstage, JEANNINE throws her apron at the mayor. She comes out from the back room wearing her coat and carrying her purse, and walks by the two guys.*

Maurice: She got to you, didn't she? I saw you over there at the garage. All starry-eyed. You let her grease your valves just so she could grab your piston. But you didn't dare invite her Saturday night 'cause deep down inside you know girls like them are afraid of sex. They're nothing but damn independent bitches.

Timothy: Well, well. I never thought of it that way, Maurice. If they're afraid of sex, they're pretty damn hypocritical!

Maurice: You better believe it!

Timothy: Yeah, I guess you're right. Can't even talk to a girl these days, can't even tell her she's good-looking, let alone take her for a ride in your car. Your own Stephanie is starting to act like that now. She can't even take a joke any more.

Maurice: Listen, Stephanie's different, OK? It's not her fault. It's just because her mother let her join the hockey team. But those girls at the garage, it wouldn't surprise me one bit if they were intending to set up a little business of their own.

Timothy: Yeah! They've already got a garage.

Maurice: That's right. First they refuse to boost our economy, and you just watch, now they're going to try to take over. I've read about women like them in the newspapers. You give them an inch and they take a mile.

Timothy: Yeah, well, Bibi can spend Saturday night alone at her garage while we have a ball at the Sex Complex.

Maurice: Now you're talking. Forget your Bibi. Forget her. You got away just in time, boy! Do you know what women like her want in their beds? An itty-bitty tenderized vegetable. That's what! And the next morning you wake up and you're practically a faggot, or almost impotent![1]

Timothy: Thanks, Maurice. Guess I didn't know which end was up for a while there.

---

1 According to the eminent Quebec sexologist Dr. Jean-Yves Desjardins, "Feminism is increasing the number of impotent men and homosexuals."

SCENE 7
Meeting of the Pink Brigades

Back to the garage. MUSIC: a slower version of the song "Miss Autobody" from the beginning of Scene 2. BIBI and BRIGITTE finish cleaning up and sit down, exhausted. The others enter from all sides, very jovial.

The music speeds up. The BRIGADES tell each other about their day and the people they met.

Bibi: Anyway, I'm not about to forget this in a hurry, believe me. I asked you to come here to give me a hand, and you end up spending the day at the beach or hanging around town. Had I known, I would've asked Mrs. Poulin. She would've come to help me.

Barbara: Hey, just a minute! We were walking around with our ears to the ground, getting the lay of the land.

Beverley: And we learned some pretty amazing things at the beach.

Brigitte: So did we, right here at the garage. This town is suffering from a serious case of mistaken identity.

Bibi: Twisted identity is more like it.

Caucus. The only audible words are "Sex Complex," heard three times.

Beatrice: A woman's right to control her own body is at stake here. We are dealing with another sex complex, but this time we're not going to be the ones to go into therapy!

Bibi: Meeting of the Pink Brigades' V-8 Cell.

All Together: BRRR!

Bibi: Here we are, on another mission in spite of ourselves. And for those of you who are wondering about the essence of our mission, let me simply say that we must increase the pressure in the tire of pornography in Pompomville until it bursts.

Beverley: We shall be the fatal nail on its "insinuous" road.

Barbara: The grain of sand in its carburetor.

Brigitte: The cup of sugar in its gas line.

All Together: Long live the flat tire!

Bibi: Work order: the re-alignment of Pompomville. The mechanics of the operation are as follows: We shall occupy the fortress of flesh in an artistic manner.

All Together: Nyaa, nyaa, nyaa.

Bibi: In a fuel-efficient but harmless manner, we shall launch Operation … Operation …

Beverley: *(suggests)* "Victorious Vaginas!"

All Together: *(hesitating)* Whaa?

Brigitte: "Infernal Vulvas!"

All Together: Huuhhhh?

Beatrice: Why not "The Charge of the Clitoridean Brigade!"

All Together: *(murmuring)* Aw no, aw no.

Barbara: No, no, no. Let's just be true to ourselves. Let's call it: "The Revenge of the Pussywillows."

All Together: *(reflective pause)* Yeah! *(They take off in various directions.)*

Bibi: Before we leave, *(they all come back)* let's reaffirm our faith in our mission. We swear …

All Together: *(hands on their own heads)* … on the head of our most cherished friend, we shall succeed. We shall flood the engines of these voyeurs.

Bibi: The Pink Brigades!

All Together: Dare! Dare! Dare! *(They run off in various directions, repeating: Dare! Dare!)*

> BARBARA *motions to* BRIGITTE *to pick up everything lying around on the floor. They whistle to imitate a conversation with questions and answers.* BARBARA *gives orders and* BRIGITTE *executes them. Tired,* BRIGITTE *exits and returns with a chair, runs out of steam and exits. The actresses do a set change in full view of the audience, transforming the garage into the kitchen at* MARIETTE *and* MAURICE's *house.*

SCENE 8
Dad and Mom

BEATRICE enters with MARIETTE slung over her shoulder and sets her up like a mannequin. BARBARA gives the signal: BRRR! The scene begins. The style is that of your favorite sitcom!

Beatrice: Thanks for the coffee. It was nice meeting you.

Mariette: Nice meeting you too, Miss Beatrice. I hope you'll stop by to see me again some time.

Beatrice: It's a promise.

BEATRICE bumps into MAURICE as he walks in.

Maurice: You've got great bumpers. I hope I didn't scare you.

Beatrice: Not at all. But if you have any dents, come to Miss Autobody!

MARIETTE laughs.

Maurice: What did she want, Mom?

Mariette: Don't you have a kiss for me, Dad? *(MAURICE gives her a distracted little kiss on the cheek.)* She just stopped by to meet me and to talk about the garage. A little courtesy visit. She seemed really nice!

Maurice: They're all over the place! How many of them are there in that garage anyway?

Mariette: Seems to be a quite few of them. I think it's great, a bunch of young people who get together to make a go of it.

Maurice: Well, not that bunch. That bunch will never make a go of it, they're never at the garage. I keep bumping into them everywhere I go. Does it take twenty-five of me to make a go of it in life, Mom?

Mariette: *(very gently)* What's the matter, Dad? Did you have a hard day? Did you have some kind of run-in with the girls?

Maurice: The girls, girls. What a way to talk. The young ladies! Next thing I know, you'll be taking sides with them!

Mariette: It's eleven fifteen, Dad.

> *MAURICE throws his hat in the air; MARIETTE catches it in mid-air and treats it like a precious object.*

Maurice: *(Fit to be ... he gets up onto the chair.)* I come home when I see fit. You wouldn't enjoy the lifestyle you enjoy if I didn't work so late. The chrome kitchen, automatic everything in every room in the house, the big car at the door so you can pick up YOUR daughter who plays HOCKEY. The way you're raising that girl, she's going to end up wandering from garage to garage.

Mariette: Come back down to earth, Dad. *(He sits down.)* Did you go over to the garage?

Maurice: Yes.

Mariette: Did you see the girls?

Maurice: Yes.

Mariette Did you do your job as volunteer fireman?

Maurice: Of course.

Mariette: Did you find anything wrong?

Maurice: No.

Mariette: *(shouts)* So why are you so upset? *(She gets carried away and crushes his hat, then, upset, she realizes her sacrilege.)*

Maurice: *(whining)* You don't understand, Mom. You could never understand, we were talking business.

Mariette: Don't tell me you offered them work at your "Sex Complex," Maurice?!

Maurice: Come on, why would I offer them work, they're not even pretty! But believe me, those girls from the garage aren't going to jeopardize twenty years of hard work. Because this time, Mom, we're not just talking about making money, we're talking about big bucks. I know some well-connected businessmen, and nobody's going to stop me this time, not even you, Mom!

Mariette: Did I ever prevent you from doing anything, Maurice! I've always supported you. But this time, I think you're investing in a strange business. It's not that I'm against it, but making money off naked girls ...

Maurice: We can't all be doctors, mom!

Kitschy, sentimental MUSIC.

Mariette: I don't understand you any more, Maurice. Ever since you got into this business, I've been afraid of losing you.

Maurice: What are you talking about, Mom!

Mariette: You're never home any more. We never see each other, Stephanie never sees you, you never talk to me any more and I feel like I never talk to you.

Maurice: That's not what you said last night, Mom! *(He squeezes her bum.)*

Mariette: *(annoyed)* You want to talk about last night, Maurice Malo?

Well, if you ask me, you act like you think you're Bruce Lee in bed. *(She removes his hand.)*

Maurice: Don't change the subject, Mom. Sex makes the world go round, and it's not my fault — that's just how things work.

Mariette: It's not your fault, but you sure as heck are taking advantage of the situation. How would you like to see Stephanie and me spend the evening at your "Sex Complex"?

Maurice: You're just confusing the issue, Mom. Places like that have to exist. I'm just providing entertainment, entertainment for men. And sometimes men need to make it fast and simple, and you're not gonna take that away from us. *(inspired tone of voice)* Besides, you might say I'm providing a social service. I'm keeping the maniacs off the streets.

Mariette: And I suppose those guys don't walk through the streets on their way home?!

MAURICE pushes back the chair, and puts his briefcase down on it. He opens the briefcase. It's a portable TV.

Maurice: You turn everything I say against me, Mom. Well, I don't care what you say. It's therapeutic. Sex therapists use these films to cure couples who are having problems.

Mariette: I guess my subconscious is different. Maybe this stuff excites some people, but it makes me uncomfortable, and ever since it's been around here, things haven't been the same between us.

MAURICE turns the TV on.

Mariette: Just what do you think you're doing, Maurice Malo?

Maurice: I'm working overtime!

Mariette: I didn't ask you to bring that into the house.

Maurice: I'm behind in my screening.

Mariette: Maurice, we had an agreement, *(lowers her voice)* and I'm not the only one in this house. What about Stephanie? I thought you had more respect for her.

Maurice: We had an agreement, Mom, but I've got my freedom too.

Mariette: Well, Maurice Malo, as of this minute, Pride has a name, it's called Woman, and I'm that woman!

> *MARIETTE takes the remote control away from him and turns the TV off. Kitschy, sentimental MUSIC, with a segue into the first heartrending "Oh, oh, oh" of the following song:*

A Man at Your Side

> *The chorus appears everywhere. First, heads appear from behind the curtains. Then little houses and clouds appear, always moving from left to right over the bar, like the continuous landscapes. Finally, we see only hands imitating big mouths. Both singers take themselves very seriously and they give a heartfelt rendition of the song, which is filled with pain and despair.*

Maurice: *(in the kitchen)*
Oh! Oh! Oh! Oh! …
I can see us at the altar
You on your father's arm
Before my brothers and God above
We promised a lifetime of love
And on our wedding night
Our nude bodies 'tween sheets so white
I gave you, I gave you a child

Chorus: Baby baby baby baby!

At last I was a man!
Yes, a man!

Just a man!
At your side!

Chorus: At your side!

Tonight you turn away from me
Stubborn as can be
You walk away so cruel
Breaking all our rules
Can't you hear my heart crying

Chorus: Baby, baby, baby, baby!

I want to be a man!
Yes a man!
Just a man
At your side!

Chorus: At your side!

Timothy: *(in the bar)*
Oh! Oh! Oh! Oh! ...
I can't drive your face
Out of the garage of my heart
I'd like to get a fresh start
But you're paranoid my love
And yet nevertheless
I see us nude between the sheets
Cruising the highway of happiness

Chorus: Baby, baby, baby, baby!

I'd like to be a man!
Yes, a man!
Just a man!
At your side!

Chorus: At your side!

Maurice and Timothy: *(standing together centrestage)*
I'm one tired Romeo
And my Juliettes are gone
Have they lost all their pity
For my lost virility?
I beg you one more time
Between the sheets be mine
And it will be, you'll see …
All that you want it to be!

Chorus: Baby, baby, baby, baby!

Just let me be a man!
Yes, a man!
Just a man!
At your side!

Chorus: At your side!

Maurice:
Oh! Oh! Oh! Oh!

> *Pause. The men prepare for the finale.*

All Together:
At your side!

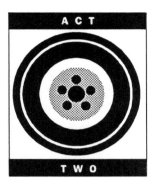

During intermission, we hear a club-like soundtrack (blues). The stage is transformed into the stage at the "Sex Complex." Centrestage, there is a plastic curtain which, given the appropriate lighting, will allow for great shadow puppet effects. On either side of the stage are two magnificent mermaids — bare-breasted, of course. The stage is lined with "chase lights" — a string of small flashing lightbulbs. The bar from the restaurant of the previous scene becomes the bar at the "Sex Complex." Behind it, a life-size inflatable doll is on display. On stage are two little poles with a red ribbon strung between them — the red ribbon to be cut at the official inauguration ceremony.

The second act actually begins during intermission with some improvised interaction with the audience. BIBI and PHEDA are seated in the audience, but not together. The improvisation between these two characters and the audience lasts about 5 minutes. The theme: Opening night at the Sex Complex in Pompomville.

Here is an example of a possible improvisation routine:

Bibi: Hello.

Someone: Hello. You're really great, good job.

Bibi: What job? Oh, that job on your car yesterday. Now I remember you, you've got that little orange Toyota, right? *(etc.)*

Pheda: Hello. Welcome to Pompomville. Tonight's the opening of Maurice's new complex. This your first time in town? I would have recognized you otherwise, I've got a good memory for faces!

The Person: Hello, what's your name?

Pheda: Pheda.

The Person: No, I mean your name in real life?

Pheda: Oh! It's Alpheda. But everyone calls me Pheda for short!

The Person Accompanying the Other Person: *(whispers)* You see, I told you she wouldn't tell you.

> *End of the sound track. End of Intermission. The KEYBOARD PLAYER enters and waves to PHEDA. She sits downs at the piano and picks up where the tape left off. The mirror ball on the ceiling starts to twirl. PHEDA sits on a stool at the bar and goes on talking while BIBI remains in the audience.*

Pheda: *(to the audience)* Did you notice the mirror ball? Pretty, eh? That was my idea! I told Maurice he should get one, but I didn't think he'd listen to me. He's a real penny-pincher! *(to the keyboard player)* Hello, Miss. *(to the audience)* So, Maurice hired a woman to play piano. Good for him! *(to the keyboard player)* Your little feather is really sweet. *(to the audience)* And they're not expensive! Oh, wow, she can play jazz. Don't you just love jazzy music? *(She dances in her seat.)*

> *TIMOTHY enters, in his fabulous sportscar as usual, acting like the "bouncer." He "brakes" and pulls up facing the bar.*

"Your little feather is really sweet."

Pheda: *(to TIMOTHY)* Oh, dear, Timothy! You've got a huge dent on your left side!

Timothy: *(panicked)* Where, where? Where?

Pheda: *(She laughs, slaps her thigh and grins at the audience.)* He falls for it every time!

> *JEANNINE sticks her head out from behind the back curtain. She's talking to MAURICE, whom we see in shadow play. Throughout the following dialogue, MAURICE's lines are replaced by sounds from the synthesizer which translate his various intentions.*

Jeannine: Maurice! Come on out, everyone's here.

Maurice: *(anxious)*

Jeannine: Yes, yes, everything's ready.

Maurice: *(questioning)*

Jeannine: Wait a minute. Yes, yes, Romeo Petit is there.

Maurice: *(proud of himself)*

Jeannine: Stop primping, your suit looks great. It's a lot nicer than the outfit you found for me!

Maurice: *(drily)*

Jeannine: All right, all right. It'll do, but if you ask me, I look like a smelt!

Maurice: *(mad)*

> *JEANNINE and MAURICE are both talking at the same time.*

Jeannine: *(mad)* Yessir! Listen, I should know!

JEANNINE enters. For our pleasure this evening, she is wearing a stunning tropical fish costume, complete with fins, a plunging neckline, a "rising tide" skirt, and sequined scales, pretty as a Chicken-of-the-Sea tuna ad. If the crowd laughs too long, she motions to some man, asking him whether he'd like to wear her costume!

Jeannine: Your speech is fine, Maurice. You rehearsed the whole thing this afternoon. You must know it by heart. See you later, I've got a job to do. *(She moves through the audience, stopping at different tables.)* Oh, I'm sorry, but this table is reserved.[1] *(She hesitates.)* You arrived a long time ago? Then just stay there, we'll work it out. Right, Timmy? *(to some individual in the crowd)* C'mon, Claude, you've known me for years. Stop gawking at me with your mouth hanging open like ... like a guppy! *(wolf whistle)* No, I don't offer room service. Just because I look like an easy catch doesn't mean I bite at any old bait. Hey, Timmy, they're pretty worked up. You think it's because it's opening night?

Timothy: *(whispering)* ... Maurice's customers.

Jeannine: Maurice's customers or not, they going to show some respect. I realize this is a tits and ass joint, but mine have work to do tonight. *(She notices the inflatable doll behind the bar.)* Timmy! What's that?

Timothy: *(whispers)* Shhh! It's courtesy of one of the sponsors.

Jeannine: Oh no! Him and his sponsors! Maurice! Maurice Malo! You're not going to get me to spend the whole evening behind my bar with some inflatable dolly. *(MAURICE growls; she resigns herself.)* They look like they're all hot to trot, Maurice. Your fan club is calling you. Maurice! Maurice!

---

1   While preparing for a performance in Rimouski, Quebec, we discovered that the local police chief was facing charges of indecent behaviour, and that the local police corps had been criticized for "subsidizing" advertising for a local striptease lounge. That night Jeannine said: "Oh sorry, but the front row is reserved for the police corps," and there was a real uproar!

*JEANNINE claps her hands and gets the audience to join her.
BIBI, TIMOTHY and PHEDA join in. Nightclub MUSIC, like
an evening with Claude Blanchard (or Liberace, depending on
where you come from).*

Timothy, Pheda, Bibi and the Audience: Maurice! Maurice!

Maurice: Is it time for me to come out, Timmy?

Timothy: Yeah ... yeah, come on out!

Entrance MUSIC.

Maurice: Good evening, ladies and gentlemen! And welcome to
opening night at the Sex Complex! It's nice to see so many of you
out there. I'd like to thank you all for joining us. I'd also like to
thank our sponsors. And many thanks to almost all of our local
businesses ...

BIBI throws balls of aluminum foil at him from the audience.

Bibi: "Almost all" is right!

Pheda: Miss Bibi! I'm over here!

Bibi: Pheda!

Pheda: Those little balls are a great idea. Have a nice evening! We're
going to have a great time! A great time!

Maurice: ... who share my definition of the word "Prosperity!" (*He
cuts the inaugural ribbon to the tune of "O Canada!,"[1] wipes a tear from his
cheek and walks into the audience to shake hands with the crowd.*) Many
thanks to the "Rumpled Silk Skin" massage parlour, thank you,
Jean-Paul. To the "Libido Bookstore," for intellectuals who prefer to
look, not touch ... Thanks, Claude! (*speaking to the same individual as at*

---

1 Or the anthem of your choice.

the beginning of the scene[1]) Many thanks to my old buddy Leopold from "The Three Knives Inn," with its bar, its aphrodisiac cuisine, its qualified rooms and its well-equipped staff. And for those who prefer solitary pleasure or wish to remain anonymous, there's the chic 7- 69, open 24 hours a day, providing "take-out" orgasms ... as well as my own "Videorotic Club" of which I am the humble President and Chief Stockholder.

Bibi: *(interrupts him)* Humble! *(She throws more balls at him.)*

Pheda: He's president of everything! Maurice Malo is president of everything in town! What else is new?!

Timothy: *(prompting MAURICE, who seems to have forgotten his speech)* And last but not least ... The Four Corners Newsstand which has just received a new shipment of those Swedish magazines ...

Maurice: ... they're on the top rack, but they're there!

Timothy: Yes, indeed ... indeed ...

Maurice: *(remembers the closing lines of his speech)* Yes, indeed. The Sex Complex is delighted to bring you a new cultural dimension ...

Bibi: Sure, sure! Long live culture!

Maurice: ... in world-class entertainment.

Pheda: World-class in Pompomville! *(She laughs.)*

Maurice: You'll see the work of great tropical artists ... *(Silver balls bombard the stage.)* Never drag out the foreplay, I always say, so without further delay, I would like to introduce my favourite M.C: Timothy "Jock" Tremblay. Let's give him a hand!

> *MAURICE runs off. PHEDA gives TIMOTHY a hand, then gets up and leaves.*

1 If some wise guy answers for real, answer him back, it's great fun. If some guy insists or becomes unpleasant, say something like: "Oh, you've brought your wife along for a change!" Usually very effective!

Timothy: *(Obviously uncomfortable on stage, he decides on the spot to tell a good joke.)* Eh? Oh, thank you, Mayor Malo. Evening everyone. Hey, do you know the one about the guy who went to a whorehouse? His buddy promises he'll wait for him in the car. "Won't be long, I know you." Ha! So there he was waiting in the car. After about half an hour, he says to himself, he's getting a bit carried away there, I'll call him. So he honks his horn — no sign of him. He waits a few more minutes, then says to himself, guess he didn't hear me, so he honks again. No sign of him. So he figures he'll really lean on the horn this time. Oops! Out comes this beautiful tall blond ... in her birthday suit ... with a mattress on her head! And she's running ... so the guy, do you believe it, the guy grabs her and asks her — *(laughing)* he asks her — *(laughing so hard he can't go on)* he asks her — *(starts laughing again)* where do you think you're going with that mattress on your head? And the girl says — *(laughing again)* she says — she says — I'm going to serve that damn fool who thinks this is a car order joint! *(He laughs really hard and, encouraged by the audience reaction, he tries again.)* You know the one about the guy who wanted to turn in the big American baby for the little Japanese job ... Got it, a big American and a little Japanese job? Well, anyway, he talks to one of his friends about it ...

> *TIMOTHY is interrupted by a pink glove which appears through the curtain, accompanied by the sound "BRRR," and hands him a piece of paper. He reads it aloud.*

"Dear Timothy, read this." *(He laughs.)* "Now I'd like to present the first act of the evening ... " *(an aside)* Go easy on the barbecue chips, the evening's going to be spicy enough. *(He laughs.)* OK, here we go, Ladies and Gentlemen, presenting ... *(He reads the slip of paper.)* Naughty Nancy! *(NANCY/BEVERLEY enters)* Miss Beverley!! Shouldn't you be over at the garage??

> *TIMOTHY runs off the stage. BEVERLEY is dressed up as a torch singer: black corset, pink lace, boas, etc. During her song, Naughty Nancy (alias BEVERLEY the Pink Brigade) purrs and growls sensually, à la Brigitte Bardot. She comes on to the audience, twisting around on her stool, and using her boa in classic striptease style.*

It's Not My Scene

Hello lover
Such a strong big boy
Hello lover
Lovin' could be a joy
If only you could change movies, lover
Cause I'm nobody's toy

In your movie I like it
With a bag over my head
In your movie I like it
When you tie me to the bed
In your movie I like it
When you shout as you please
In your movie I like it
When you force me to my knees

For centuries now
There's something I don't get
All those tricks and scenes
In your sad film noir
Yet I still believe that sex can be so fine
But pain, pain is your scene, not mine

Say we were to change places
And despite your desperate cries
I whipped you through the paces
Or tickled you till you cried
Thinking that you liked it, like that

What if my own pleasure rose
Despite your cries and pleas
By shoving the vacuum cleaner hose
Up your bum while you're on your knees
Thinking that you like it, like that
Why is everything frenetic
So empty and pathetic
That desire must be stolen
Or purchased pre-prepared
Thinking that we like it, like that

And the moral of this story
If I draw my conclusions
Is that despite popular belief, women
Are neither tigresses nor pigs

Hello lover
Such a strong big boy
Sorry lover
If there's pain, there's no joy
Sorry but it's not my scene!

Bibi: *(first from the audience, then on stage)* Timmy! Where are you? Tim!
(She sees the shape of his car behind the curtain. We hear grumbling.) Is this
where you wanted to take me on Saturday night? No! Too bad! I really
like this show! Aren't you going to come out and introduce the next act?
(We hear the sound of Timothy's car driving away.) The dancers are
ready. Ladies and Gentlemen, welcome to CLOSING night at the Sex
Complex! Now, Miss Autobody is delighted to present, directly from
the Island of Lesbos, an erotic couple, in the finest tradition. And now,
in their act "Human Pussycats," I'd like to introduce, Savory and
Marjoram!

> *Two PINK BRIGADES enter, dressed up as ethereal nymphs.*
> *They don't walk, they fly! They scatter little pieces of paper to the*
> *four winds, like so many rose petals! Ingenuous, dumb and cute,*
> *à la David Hamilton.*

When Two Pretty Girls
or "Human Pussycats"

Without us no show
Is erotic or complete
We add spice and a glow
We make a meal a treat

It gets everybody going
Both over and under thirty
When two pretty girls (repeat)
Play the dirty-gurdy

The Keyboard Player: The what?

The Singers: The dirty-gurdy!

Without us no cure
Could be tempting or complete
We are love's delinquents
Our neuroses are so neat
Everyone finds it so intriguing
Though something they're above
When two pretty girls *(repeat)*
Decide to fall in love

Without us no show
Is friendly and erotic
Cause all men think they can cure
A lady's who's neurotic
They all dream of trying
Both over and under thirty
When two pretty girls *(repeat)*
Play the dirty-gurdy

Jeannine: The what?

The Singers: The dirty-gurdy!

Without us no church
Could damn erotic union
And allow us no communion,
Just burning at the stake

Now everyone shouts scandal
Something they can't handle
When two pretty girls *(repeat)*
Decide to fall in love

Without us, no show
Can be truly erotic
We're the scientific dimension
You can really feel the tension
When everyone tries to measure
Is there any true pleasure
When two pretty girls *(repeat)*
Play the dirty-gurdy

The Keyboard Player and Jeannine: The what?

The Singers: The dirty-gurdy!

When two pretty girls *(repeat)*
Decide to fall in love.

    They exit.

Maurice: *(in the audience)* Timothy? Timothy? I'm warning you, if you've left, you're fired! *(really mad)* Jeannine! What do you think you're doing? Help me. Tell those two wise-cracking girls from the garage their little joke is over. And grab that Miss Bibi and throw her out! On the double!

Jeannine: That's not my job. I'm not your bouncer!

Maurice: You get paid to keep your mouth shut and do what I say!

Jeannine: *(getting mad, and pointing to the inflatable doll.)* Like her?

    *Strident noise. JEANNINE heads toward MAURICE holding
    the inflatable doll. He backs away, out of the light. Then to the
    MUSIC of a Chopin Nocturne, JEANNINE moves to the center
    of the stage, twirling gracefully with the doll. They waltz briefly.*

While looking at the audience, JEANNINE holds the doll in her arms, as if to protect her from them. Then she leaves the doll standing upstage and starts to sing. It's a sad country-western song, accompanied on the accordion. She sings the choruses to the doll and the verses to the audience. She dresses the doll in a sheet during the second chorus. During the third verse, an actress takes the place of the inflatable doll. She too is draped in a sheet and stands in the same position, with gaping mouth, eyes wide open, arms stretched out. JEANNINE goes back to the actress-doll and dances gently with her. She puts her arm around her neck and slowly leads her to the bar. At the end of the song, we hear the same strident noise again. Blackout on stage. Lights. Everything is in the same position as before the song. We realize that the scene has taken place in JEANNINE's imagination.

The Waitress and the Doll

Chorus:

Oh! my baby, oh! my sweetheart
Your gaping mouth is like my life
Oh! my baby, oh! my sweetheart
From your gaping mouth there's no cry of love

Waitress I am
Waitress I'm proud to be
I like my customers
And my customers like me
When they start actin' crazy
I can always talk them down
Tonight I wish I was
Back working behind my bar

Chorus: Oh! my baby ...

When he disguised me
It was pretty bad
But when it's boss's orders
You just try getting mad

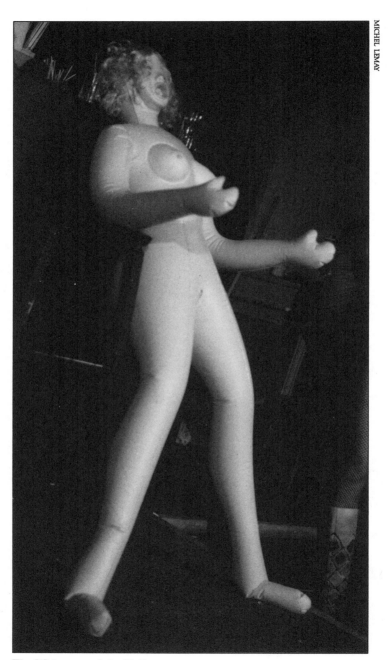

The Waitress and the Doll

You don't like it, they kick you out
Tonight I wish I was
Back working behind my bar

I work all the tables
And I'm not ashamed
I thought that respect
Was what I'd claimed
Like you I'm inflated
Bursting with anger
Tonight I wish I was
Back working behind my bar

Chorus: Oh! my baby ...

Waitress I am
Waitress I'm proud to be
There must be somewhere
In this world
A place where pleasure
Is less bruised
Tonight I'm opening
The lounge of my life

> *JEANNINE is behind the bar with the inflatable doll, exactly as she was before the song.*

Maurice: You get paid to keep your mouth shut and do what I say.

Jeannine: *(mad)* Like her?

> *Total change of atmosphere achieved by the playful MUSIC from "Human Pussycats" and PHEDA's sudden arrival on stage.*

Pheda: *(arriving from backstage)* Wow! What fun! So much action! Real action! I didn't know night life could be this exciting! So, Maurice, this is what a sex joint is like?

Maurice: With all due respect, Mrs. Simard, get lost! Disappear!

Pheda: What do you mean disappear? I thought we were supposed to have fun in a place like this?

Maurice: It's no place for a woman your age. You should be at home in bed.

Pheda: You can't send me to bed at ten fifteen, with a little kiss on the forehead. Are you kidding!? I've been going to bed late all my life. *(to the audience)* Ladies and Gentlemen, I'd like to ask you for a few more minutes of your time. And now for what you might call the dessert of the evening. In fact, I'm really proud that she asked me to introduce her! Ladies and Gentlemen: "The Desert Vixen."

> *MARIETTE enters, dressed as a "genie" (à la Barbara Eden's character in the 1960s TV show "I Dream of Jeannie") with see-through veils, harem pants, flashy jewellery and a veil over her face.*

Nymphomania

> *MARIETTE hypnotizes MAURICE as he heads toward her. She falls into his arms singing:*

Mariette:
Nymphomania, nymphomania
Yes it's me the lovely desert vixen
Nymphomania, nymphomania
When I dance even the camels lose their cool
Nymphomania, nymphomania
Let me lead the caravan of your desires
Nymphomania, nymphomania
Just hurry, come join me in my casbah

> *MAURICE raises the veil and recognizes his wife.*

Maurice: *(incredulous)* Mom? Oh, no! Not my mother, not my wife!
(The beat becomes more "rock'n'roll.") Oh, no! Not my daughter, not my
sister!

Mariette:
Oh, yes! Not your mother, not your wife?
Oh, yes! Not your daughter, not your sister?
So who's going to dance, who's going to shake it baby? *(repeat)*

Pheda: *(speaking)* Just leave it to me, I'll show 'em how!

She stands up on her barstool and starts shakin' it.

Mariette and a Veiled Pink Brigade:
Nymphomania, nymphomania
Yes, it's me, the lovely desert vixen
Nymphomania, nymphomania
When I dance, the wild beasts fall at my feet

*JEANNINE and PHEDA join in the belly-dancing. They're
having a great time and they too have put veils over their faces —
JEANNINE uses her dishrag and PHEDA, her lace collar.*

Nymphomania, nymphomania
Let me drown you in oriental caresses
Nymphomania, nymphomania
Let me show you my jewel of a belly button.

MAURICE tries to take MARIETTE away. She resists.

MAURICE and MARIETTE sing at the same time:

Maurice:
Oh, no! Not my mother, not my wife!
Oh, no! Not my daughter, not my sister!

Mariette:
Oh, yes! Not your mother, not your wife?
Oh, yes! Not your daughter, not your sister?

"Yes, it's me, the lovely desert vixen / When I dance, the wild beasts fall at my feet ..."

They all take off their veils and they get more excited.

All the Women:
Who's going to dance, who's going to shake it baby!? *(three times)*

Pheda And Jeannine: *(speaking during above)* Did you say dance, Mariette?! Here we come! It's partytime! Yahoo!

All the Women:
Nymphomania, nymphomania
Yes, it's me, the lovely vixen of your youth
Nymphomania, nymphomania
You've taken the giddiness from my dances
Nymphomania, nymphomania
You make me flee the harem of your caresses
Nymphomania, nymphomania
Off with the veil, the veil that disguised our love.

> *The women exit. When everyone has left the stage, PHEDA reappears and dances over to MAURICE.*

Pheda: Mariette! Aren't you glad we took those aerobic dance classes?! *(notices MAURICE is shattered)* Come on, Maurice! Don't take it personally, take it historically, take it historically!

Mariette: *(reappears on stage and freezes in a pose)* Now that I know how you see me, Maurice Malo, just imagine how I see you.

> *MAURICE runs over to her and freezes in a pose. They look like a monument.*

Maurice: Mom!

Offstage Voice: *(in classical narration style)* What will become of Mariette and Maurice? Will their love survive? Will their daughter Stephanie get to play for the Nordiques?

Maurice: *(pleading)* Mom!

The monument exits to the same kitschy, sentimental MUSIC heard in Scene 8. PHEDA leaves the bar and walks back onto the stage.

Pheda: Ladies and Gentlemen, it's me again! I heard through the grapevine that Maurice wanted to end the evening with a movie, a beautiful love story! That's right, so here is what you might call "the cherry on the Sundae."

She pulls down a movie screen, for the presentation of brief excerpts from pornographic films. The montage begins with images of strippers, progressing to scenes of wide-eyed women being chained and handcuffed, to horrifying images of women having electrodes applied to their nipples. During the projection, the actresses hum the music of the final song, and begin to sing once the film has ended.

Women Touch Me

Shame, shame is a feeling
That cannot be shared
Women touch me

A sadness so great that
Not a single sob is heard
Women touch me

The sound of pain has never
Even travelled through time
Women touch me

Love! With twisted roots so deep
You will fill all our gardens
With flowers so hideous and ugly
With petals torn and scarred
Women touch me

Love! When truth vies with vanity
You will fill all our hearts
With dreams so mean and shrivelled

Your essence will remain unknown
Women touch me

Love! Poets refuse to believe you
To me they sound delirious
And they cover with scorn
The women that I cry for
Women touch me

Each new morning they must bathe
In the warm water of their tears
Then they don the bitter jewels
Forged in their sadness and pain
Women touch me

From their closet of bitterness
They take their finest clothes
Just to cover up their suffering
In courage fine as velvet
Women touch me

They can face the storms of life
Like a ship's maiden voyage
Because they shall always believe
In Love.

Women touch me.
Women touch me.
Women touch me.

THE END

Afterword

From the very outset, we knew that we would show some hardcore pornography in *Mademoiselle Autobody*.[1] There was no avoiding it. *Otherwise we ran the risk of trivializing the subject.* Yes, we wanted to make people laugh, but we wanted to disturb them and provoke their awareness as well. To put it bluntly, *we believe that the play should not be performed without this ending.* Laughing at pornography and violence against women in absolutely unacceptable unless that laughter is used as bait and becomes caustic and denunciatory. The power of the film presentation comes from the fact that there is no distance between the spectators and the material. It leaves the men and women in the audience alone with the film. The actresses are no longer on stage, and there are no images of people consuming pornography: the audience members are left watching the film themselves.

Our incomprehension in the face of the hatred towards women inherent in pornography was fully shared by audiences when they watched the film excerpts. Such images are worth thousands of words. The impact of the screening was overwhelming. Its length was calculated down to the second. Any shorter, and it would have been little more than a fleeting glimpse; any longer, and it would have become torture.

This montage should be shorter than the last song. In our production, the projection began in silence and gradually a soundtrack was introduced: our voices behind the screen humming the melody of the closing song. The audience will feel as if the film lasts forever. It is important not to end the show on that note—the shock is too great. The actresses come back onto the stage with a song of love and the hope of love. At the end of the song, as they sing the refrain "women touch me" one last time, the actresses join hands, creating a human chain which projects an incredible sense of solidarity and strength. Once again, an image is worth a thousand words.

Ending the play in this way strengthens the link between theatre and real life. And, as you know by now, that's the way les Folles Alliées like it!

---

1 The movie we used was a montage of pornographic films used in the documentary "Not a Love Story," by Bonnie Sherr Klein and Dorothy Hénault, produced by the National Film Board of Canada. We recommend that those wishing to produce *Miss Autobody* create their own film montage based on material found in their own community.

Ze Girls On Vacation

Miss Autobody

Pheda's Song

percussion instruments
de
cuisine!

al $.

fine

Boys Will Be Boys

Which End Is Up?

A Man at Your Side

It's Not My Scene

When Two Pretty Girls
or "Human Pussycats"

Fine

The Waitress and the Doll

Nymphomania

fin

Women Touch Me

fine

Also from gynergy books

By Word of Mouth: Lesbians Write the Erotic, *Lee Fleming (ed.)*. " ... contains plenty of sexy good writing and furthers the desperately needed honest discussion of what we mean by 'erotic' and by 'lesbian'." SINISTER WISDOM
ISBN 0-921881-06-1 $10.95/$12.95 US

Each Small Step: Breaking the Chains of Abuse and Addiction, *Marilyn MacKinnon (ed.)*. This groundbreaking anthology contains narratives by women recovering from the traumas of childhood sexual abuse and alcohol and chemical dependency.
ISBN 0-921881-17-7 $10.95

Fascination and Other Bar Stories, *Jackie Manthorne*. These are satisfying stories of the rituals of seduction and sexuality. "A funny and hot collection from the smoky heart of the Montreal bar beat." SINISTER WISDOM
ISBN 0-921881-16-9 $9.95

Friends I Never Knew, *Tanya Lester*. In this finely crafted novel, Tara exiles herself on a Greek island to write about five extraordinary women she has met from her years in the women's movement. In the process, Tara unexpectedly writes her own story.
ISBN 0-921881-18-5 $10.95

A House Not Her Own: Stories from Beirut, *Emily Nasrallah*. "For centuries we've been seeing war through men's eyes. Nasrallah's unflinching yet compassionate prose presents it through the eyes of women." BOOKS IN CANADA
ISBN 0-921881-19-3 $12.95

Imprinting Our Image: An International Anthology by Women with Disabilities, *Diane Driedger and Susan Gray (eds.)*. "In this global tour de force, 30 writers from 17 countries provide dramatic insight into a wide range of issues germane to both the women's and disability rights movements." DISABLED PEOPLES' INTERNATIONAL
ISBN 0-921881-22-3 $12.95

Lesbians Ignited, *Carolyn Gammon*. This impassioned first book of poetry delves into the fiery heart of lesbian life and love. "Gammon's work is a positive representation and celebration of female sexuality." WLW JOURNAL
ISBN 0-921881-21-5 $9.95

The Montreal Massacre, Marie Chalouh and Louise Malette (eds.). Feminist letters, essays, and poems examine the misogyny inherent in the mass murder of fourteen women at Ecole Polytechnique in Montreal, Quebec on December 6, 1989.
ISBN 0-921881-14-2 $12.95

Tide Lines: Stories of Change by Lesbians, Lee Fleming (ed.). These diverse short stories explore the many faces of change — instantaneous, over-a-lifetime, subtle or cataclysmic.
ISBN 0-921881-15-0 $10.95

Triad Moon, Gillean Chase. Meet Lila, Brook and Helen, three women whose bonds of love take them beyond conventional relationships. *Triad Moon* is an exhilarating read that skilfully explores past and present lives, survival from incest, and healing.
ISBN 0-921881-28-2 $9.95

Without Wings, Jackie Manthorne. In this new collection of interwoven stories, the author of *Fascination and Other Bar Stories* moves her characters out of the bar and into life. With wry humour, Manthorne creates an eminently readable tale of lesbian life today.
ISBN 0-921881-29-0 $9.95

Woman in the Rock, Claudia Gahlinger. A haunting collection of stories about forgetting and remembering incest by an award-winning writer. Gahlinger's characters live near the sea and find consolation in fishing, an act that allows for the eventual, triumphant emergence of the "woman in the rock."
ISBN 0-921881-26-6 $10.95/$9.95 US

Where Once Our Mothers Stood We Stand: Women's Suffrage in New-foundland, 1890-1925, Margot I. Duley. In this important and lively book, the rich history of the women's suffrage movement in Newfoundland is uncovered. Duley draws on diverse sources and includes fascinating interviews with descendants and friends of the suffragists.
ISBN 0-921881-24-X $12.95

gynergy books is distributed in Canada by General Publishing, by InBook in the U.S. and in the U.K. by Turnaround. Individual orders can be sent, prepaid, to: gynergy books, P.O. Box 2023, Charlottetown, PEI, Canada, C1A 7N7. Please add postage and handling ($2.00 for the first book and .75 for each additional book) to your order. Canadian residents add 7% GST to the total amount. GST registration number R104383120.